MW01503822

First paperback edition March 2023

Design by Nicole Jacobsmeyer

What to expect...

I'm so glad you picked up this resource to help you discover purpose in your pain. I pray that both this workbook and *Take Back Your Joy* bring you into a deeper relationship with Christ...one of healing, freedom, and joy.

From coloring pages and reflection questions to gratitude and action items, you will have something different *every* day to keep you pressing into Christ and meditating on His Word.

So, grab some friends to do this with you or savor your time alone with the Lord. Keep going, sweet friend. Life is tough...but so are you because you have the only ONE in you who can heal, redeem, and restore your life.

All for His glory,

Nicole

contents

week one
GROUNDED

Happy Monday
Happy Monday
Happy Monday
Happy Monday
Happy Monday
Happy Monday
Happy Monday
Happy Monday

MONDAY GRATITUDE

TODAY I'M FEELING

I'M THANKFUL FOR THE BIBLE BECAUSE...

TODAY I'M GRATEFUL FOR

1 _____

2 _____

3 _____

SOMETHING I'M WORKING ON...

MORE OF THIS:

LESS OF THIS:

I AM BLESSED BECAUSE...

TOMORROW I LOOK FORWARD TO

tuesday
DEVOTIONAL

SAVED BY SCRIPTURE

I'm going to be honest with you: I am terrible at memorizing Scripture. Even my kids are better at it than I am, which probably just means I'm getting old. But I'm working hard at Scripture memorization because I know that when trials come, the only words I can turn to for peace, comfort, and wisdom are from Christ.

However, if we don't even open our Bibles, how will we fill our minds with the truth? If I go through a season where I'm not in the Word and I'm faced with a difficult trial, I stress-eat chocolate chip cookies, I call a friend and complain, I let anger and bitterness take root in my heart. In other words, I'm all over the place. But when I'm grounded and rooted in the Word, I'm a completely different person. It's like the pain is softened and I'm able to see the bigger picture of God at work in my life because I know He loves me and is working behind the scenes on my behalf.

When we have the Word as our daily bread, we can combat the enemy's lies. The truth seeps into our hearts and minds, allowing us to speak truth when it matters most, pray boldly for others, and declare God's promises over our own lives. I challenge you today to DIG into the Bible. Study. Sit with a verse. Memorize it. Let the power of the Word be what carries you through.

Keep going, friend.

KEY VERSES

2 Corinthians 5:17, Philippians 2:16-18, Deuteronomy 8:3, Ephesians 6:17

wednesday prayer

THURSDAY JOURNAL DAY

PROMPT: HOW HAS GOD'S WORD TRANSFORMED ME?

VERSE TO MEDITATE ON

HONEST THOUGHT

CREATIVE FRIDAY

"For the Word of God is living and active, sharper than any two-edged sword, piercing to the division of soul and of spirit, of joints and of marrow, and discerning the thoughts and intentions of the heart."
Hebrews 4:12 ESV

saturday
action item

MEMORIZE A BIBLE VERSE

Pick a verse that's been on your heart lately and start memorizing it today. Or challenge yourself and make it a whole paragraph! All I know is that the older we get, the harder memorization becomes so let's today!

check when complete

Sunday Reflections

WOULD YOU CONSIDER YOURSELF ROOTED IN THE WORD OF GOD OR ARE YOU LED MORE BY YOUR EMOTIONS AND FEELINGS? EXPLAIN.

_____

_____

_____

_____

WHAT CAN YOU WORK ON TODAY/THIS WEEK TO HAVE A MORE SOLID FOUNDATION IN CHRIST?

_____

_____

_____

_____

WHAT TRANSLATION OF THE BIBLE DO YOU USE AND WHY?

_____

_____

_____

_____

WHAT IS YOUR FAVORITE TRUTH ABOUT GOD'S WORD? (EX: TRANSFORMATIONAL, UNCHANGING, INSPIRED, POWERFUL...)

_____

_____

_____

_____

week two
TRUTH

Happy Monday
Happy Monday
Happy Monday
Happy Monday
Happy Monday
Happy Monday
Happy Monday
Happy Monday

MONDAY GRATITUDE

TODAY I'M FEELING

GOD IS...

TODAY I'M GRATEFUL FOR

1
2
3

SOMETHING I'M WORKING ON...

MORE OF THIS:

LESS OF THIS:

I AM BLESSED BECAUSE...

I LOVE THE LORD BECAUSE...

tuesday
DEVOTIONAL

SANCTIFIED THROUGH SUFFERING

When life is hard, it can be overwhelming. The pain and stress affects our relationships, especially with those closest to us. After I endured a series of painful events including rape, cancer, and miscarriage, I had a distorted view of God. I couldn't trust Him after He allowed me to experience such pain. I had no idea how to heal. And I didn't know how to move forward and trust in my relationship with God.

What I now understand is that each of the trials I have walked through have not ultimately pushed me away from Him. I may have been angry and questioning in different seasons, but those trials have given me a better understanding of His character. By His great love He has rescued me, redeemed me, healed me, and fostered my growth. He has produced in me an endurance that will keep me going when all seems lost. Not by my strength, but by His.

Trials make us more like His Son, which is all we could ask. It's painful and not enjoyable. I will never like trials, but they produce the traits we pray for: peace, wisdom, grace, kindness, joy. They conform us to His image, sanctify us through suffering, and allow us to partner with Him to reach the lost through our own testimonies. And the best part is that He is unchanging and always there, ready to pour out His grace and love. We serve the only One who can heal and redeem and restore what was left shattered and broken in our lives. Oh, how grateful I am for our God, full of faithfulness and goodness and mercy and love.

Can you say the same?

KEY VERSES
Psalm 86:15, Isaiah 26:3, Romans 8:27-39, 1 John 1:9

wednesday prayer

THURSDAY JOURNAL DAY

PROMPT: DO I BELIEVE GOD IS GOOD?

VERSE TO MEDITATE ON

HONEST THOUGHT

CREATIVE FRIDAY

"Do not be frightened, and do not be dismayed, for the LORD your God is with you wherever you go." Joshua 1:9 ESV

saturday
action item

GO ON A WALK

Put some music on, put the kids in a stroller, or simply go alone and enjoy the peace of being outside. Soak in the vitamin D, take a deep breath, exhale all the problems of the day and meditate on His faithfulness.

"Great is his faithfulness; his mercies begin afresh each morning."
Lamentations 3:23 NLT

check when complete

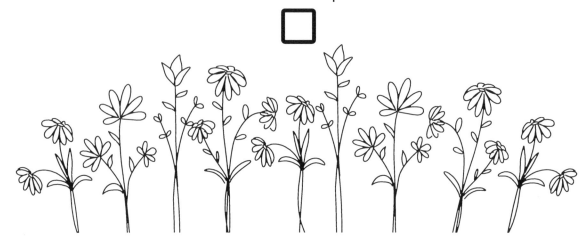

Sunday Reflections

DO YOU BELIEVE GOD IS WHO HE SAYS HE IS?
IF SO, HOW DO YOU LIVE IT OUT?

_____

_____

_____

_____

WHAT'S THE DIFFERENCE BETWEEN BEING HAPPY AND BEING JOYFUL?

_____

_____

_____

_____

WHO IS GOD TO YOU?

_____

_____

_____

_____

WHAT HAS GOD GIVEN YOU THAT THE ENEMY IS AFTER?
(RECOGNIZING THIS HELPS COMBAT THE ENEMY'S PLANS)

_____

_____

_____

week three
FORGIVE

Happy *Monday*
Happy *Monday*
Happy *Monday*
Happy *Monday*
Happy *Monday*
Happy *Monday*
Happy *Monday*
Happy *Monday*

MONDAY GRATITUDE

TODAY I'M FEELING

WHO DOES GOD SAY I AM?

TODAY I'M GRATEFUL FOR

1
2
3

SOMETHING I'M WORKING ON...

MORE OF THIS:

LESS OF THIS:

I AM BLESSED BECAUSE...

WHAT CAN I LET GO OF TODAY?

DEVOTIONAL

FORGIVENESS LEADS TO FREEDOM

I have a very difficult time doing the right thing when it feels uncomfortable, messy, or hard. I wish that wasn't the case and I could tell you that I find it easy to follow all of the Lord's commands. But, that's just not true. Forgiving someone who has deeply wronged me is something I have really struggled with.

I've had to forgive countless people who betrayed me, lied to me, gossiped about me, rejected me, and violated me. It's easy to forgive when the offense isn't personal or that big of a deal. But when it alters your life, affects those around you, keeps you up at night, or continually haunts you, it feels virtually impossible to forgive. That's why I believe Jesus talked about forgiveness so often because He knows an unforgiving heart will lead to a bitter, angry, and depressed life. That's not how God designed us to live.

We must forgive in order to live free. All sins done to us or committed by us are ultimately against God. Because of that, we will all stand and give an account before a just God on judgement day. We need to be set free from burdens like unforgiveness that aren't ours to bear. Throw it off, forgive, and live free today.

KEY VERSES

Romans 12:19, Psalm 51:4-5, Ephesians 4:32, James 1:9

wednesday prayer

THURSDAY JOURNAL DAY

PROMPT: WHO DO I NEED TO FORGIVE SO THAT I CAN LIVE FREE?

_____

_____

_____

_____

_____

_____

_____

_____

_____

_____

_____

_____

_____

_____

_____

_____

_____

VERSE TO MEDITATE ON

HONEST THOUGHT

CREATIVE FRIDAY

"Father, forgive them, for they know
not what they do."
Luke 23:34 ESV

saturday
action item

SING WAY TOO LOUD

There is something about worshiping or dancing and singing in the kitchen, or even crying to a sad song, that is so freeing. This week has been heavy because forgiving those who have wronged you is flat out difficult. Today, let it out. Dance, sing, weep, journal, go for a drive, or play your favorite song on repeat. Whatever helps you get past the hurdle of forgiving that person who wronged you, do it today. Don't let one more day go by where you're harboring resentment and unforgiveness. It's time to sing and be free!

check when complete

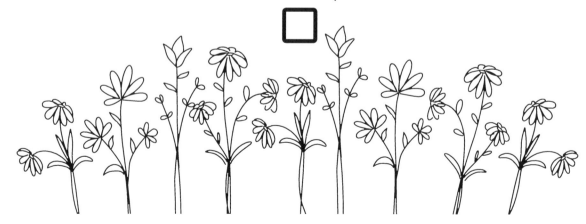

Sunday Reflections

HAVE YOU TRULY FORGIVEN THE PEOPLE IN YOUR LIFE WHO HAVE HURT
YOU? IF NOT, WHAT'S HOLDING YOU BACK?

_____

_____

_____

_____

ARE WE REALLY SUPPOSED TO FORGIVE EVERYONE? HOW DO YOU KNOW?

_____

_____

_____

_____

WHAT IS A VERSE ON FORGIVENESS THAT YOU CAN MEDITATE ON TODAY?

_____

_____

_____

_____

HOW DOES FORGIVENESS LEAD YOU TO JOY?

_____

_____

_____

_____

week four
SERVE

Happy Monday
Happy Monday
Happy Monday
Happy Monday
Happy Monday
Happy Monday
Happy Monday
Happy Monday

MONDAY GRATITUDE

TODAY I'M FEELING

WHO CAN I SERVE THIS WEEK?

TODAY I'M GRATEFUL FOR

1.
2.
3.

SOMETHING I'M WORKING ON...

MORE OF THIS:

LESS OF THIS:

I AM BLESSED BECAUSE...

tuesday
DEVOTIONAL

WITH EVERY SEASON

There is a season for everything. A season to rest and a season to run. A season to fight and a season to heal. A season to speak and a season to listen. When we are filled with the Holy Spirit, it is easier to discern the season that we are in. This is especially important after trauma or suffering. We have to be in step with the Spirit, knowing our journey may not be the same as those around us.

For years after being raped, I didn't know what season I was in because my mind was swirling, full of chaos and pain. I felt like I didn't have a purpose. But God used a season of service and leading a mission trip to renew my strength and faith in the One who could mend my brokenness. God had me focus on others instead of myself. He rescued me. Maybe not as fast as I wanted or in the way I expected. But, ultimately, He lifted me up and put my feet on solid ground. That is what our God does!

So if you're in a season of hurt or pain, ask the Holy Spirit to show you what you need to do. Do you need to rest? Set boundaries? Heal? Get counseling? Get off social media? Serve? Whatever it is, do it. But make sure you take the time to look at the people around you, because serving them might be the missing puzzle piece to your healing process.

KEY VERSES
Matthew 20:28, Ecclesiastes 3, Colossians 3:23

wednesday prayer

THURSDAY JOURNAL DAY

PROMPT: SERVING BRINGS ME JOY BECAUSE...

VERSE TO MEDITATE ON

HONEST THOUGHT

CREATIVE FRIDAY

"For who is greater, the one who is at the table or the one who serves? Is it not the one who is at the table? But I am among you as one who serves." Luke 22:27 NIV

saturday
action item

BRING A FRIEND COFFEE

Do something for someone else today. Not everyone shares their struggles, so pray and ask the Lord who in your inner circle needs an extra dose of love or encouragement. Others need to know that they are not forgotten in the chaos and pain of life. I understand how hard this action item is when you're hurting. Let's try to focus on someone else today, even if it's just for a moment.

check when complete

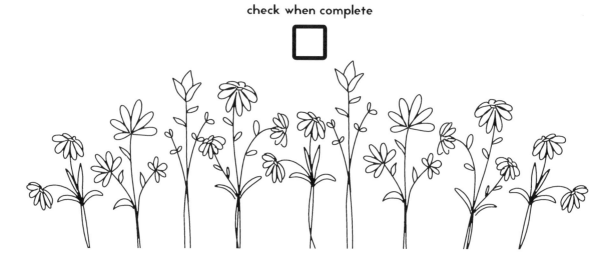

Sunday Reflections

HAS GOD EVER USED SERVICE/SERVING OTHERS AS PART OF YOUR HEALING PROCESS? IF SO, HOW DID IT HELP?

_____

_____

_____

_____

DO YOU GIVE YOURSELF THE SAME AMOUNT OF GRACE YOU GIVE TO OTHERS?

_____

_____

_____

_____

HOW CAN YOU BECOME A SERVING LEADER?

_____

_____

_____

_____

WHAT IS YOUR FAVORITE VERSE ON GRACE, SECOND CHANCES, OR SERVICE?

_____

_____

_____

_____

week five
SHIFT

Happy Monday
Happy Monday
Happy Monday
Happy Monday
Happy Monday
Happy Monday
Happy Monday
Happy Monday

MONDAY GRATITUDE

TODAY I'M FEELING

WRITE A FEW THINGS DOWN ABOUT THE
GOODNESS OF GOD...

TODAY I'M GRATEFUL FOR

1
2
3

SOMETHING I'M WORKING ON...

MORE OF THIS:	LESS OF THIS:

I AM BLESSED BECAUSE...

I LOVE...

tuesday
DEVOTIONAL

ANOTHER CAR LINE

I was sitting in yet another car line, waiting for my kids to get out of school. It was one of those days when the "mom life" was starting to take a toll on me. I started adding up all of the time that I spent each and every day waiting on everyone in my family. Making breakfast, packing lunches, planning dinners, driving back and forth, sitting in the car, wiping bottoms, cleaning bathrooms. I was frustrated. Maybe I needed some change in my life, a new season, clarity, excitement...something more.

What I was failing to see was that the goodness of God was all around me. I had four kids to love, a new home, a loving husband, a car that reliably gets us from point A to point B, and healthy food to feed our family. While we're not rich by any stretch of the imagination, I am eternally rich because of my relationship with Christ and the blessings that He has given me. Sometimes, I wonder if God is waiting for us to find our contentment in Him and what He has already given us before He gives us extra. We don't live for the "extra" but I've found that to often be true in my own life.

When we see our life through the world's eyes, it's easy to be discouraged and not content. Having an eternal perspective and a heart full of praise will always help us to be content with the life God has given us. Keep going, friends, and remind yourself to take a step back and view your life through God's lens.

KEY VERSES
Colossians 3:2, 1 Peter 5:10, Matthew 11:29

wednesday prayer

THURSDAY JOURNAL DAY

PROMPT: LIST OUT EVERY GOOD THING IN YOUR LIFE

VERSE TO MEDITATE ON

HONEST THOUGHT

CREATIVE FRIDAY

"The Lord is my strength and my song, and He has become my salvation; this is my God, and I will praise Him." Exodus 15:2 NASB

saturday

action item

NO SOCIAL MEDIA TODAY

We ALL know how social media can get us in a
negative head space at times. So today, take a day
off. Enjoy what you have right in front of you. Be
grateful for what God is doing in your life today.
Use your time wisely and maybe take tomorrow off
of social media, too, or even the entire month!

check when complete

Sunday Reflections

WHAT ARE YOU BLESSED WITH?

_____

_____

_____

_____

DO YOU BELIEVE GOD IS IN YOUR MIDST, ALWAYS WORKING BEHIND THE
SCENES? IF SO, HOW DO YOU KNOW? IF NOT, WHY?

_____

_____

_____

IN WHAT WAYS HAVE YOU SEEN GOD'S FAITHFULNESS?

_____

_____

_____

WHAT VERSE CAN YOU MEMORIZE AND MEDITATE ON THIS WEEK ABOUT
GOD'S GOODNESS?

_____

_____

_____

week six
REST

Happy Monday
Happy Monday
Happy Monday
Happy Monday
Happy Monday
Happy Monday
Happy Monday
Happy Monday

MONDAY GRATITUDE

TODAY I'M FEELING

WHAT DOES GOD SAY ABOUT REST?

TODAY I'M GRATEFUL FOR

1. _____
2. _____
3. _____

SOMETHING I'M WORKING ON...

MORE OF THIS:	LESS OF THIS:

I AM BLESSED BECAUSE...

HOW CAN YOU TAKE A DEEP BREATH AND REST TODAY?

tuesday
DEVOTIONAL

IT'S DIFFICULT BUT IT'S WORTH IT

I am not a fan of resting. I hate the thought of "taking a day off." I'm sure someone who is reading this also gets an uncomfortable feeling when they are forced to pause. While I had to learn that there are seasons for rest while I had cancer, I still find it very difficult to pause or take a breath.

In Matthew 11:28, Jesus says, "Come to me, all who are weary and burdened, and I will give you rest." Sometimes when I hear this verse, I think, "But bills still need to be paid!" I know that I probably shouldn't have told you that, but the truth is that we often get so wrapped up in our own lives that we misunderstand what God is asking of us. Rest doesn't mean I lock myself in my room, shirk all my responsibilities, and leave my kids to fend for themselves (which actually sounds really stressful). What Jesus is telling us is that our souls can be at rest, even in the midst of chaos. We can rest in Him, knowing that all will be made right, He loves us unconditionally, we have nothing to prove, and that a glorious eternity with our Creator lies ahead. We can rest as we stand on the truth of who God is: faithful, just, loving, and gracious.

Take your burdens off and lay them at His feet. He can shoulder it.

KEY VERSES
Genesis 2:2-3, Luke 10:38-42, John 14:27

wednesday prayer

THURSDAY JOURNAL DAY

PROMPT: WHY DO I FEEL THE NEED TO KEEP GOING WHEN REST IS NEEDED?

_____

_____

_____

_____

_____

_____

_____

_____

_____

_____

_____

_____

_____

_____

_____

_____

_____

VERSE TO MEDITATE ON

HONEST THOUGHT

CREATIVE FRIDAY

"For God alone my soul waits in silence; from him comes my salvation.
He alone is my rock and my salvation, my fortress; I shall not
be greatly shaken."
Pslam 62:1-2 ESV

saturday
action item

ALLOW SILENCE

Make room for peace. For rest. For stillness. For God to speak. For calm. Aim for 10-15 minutes of uninterrupted silence today.

"And the peace of God, which transcends all understanding, will guard your hearts and your minds in Christ Jesus."
Philippians 4:7 NIV

check when complete

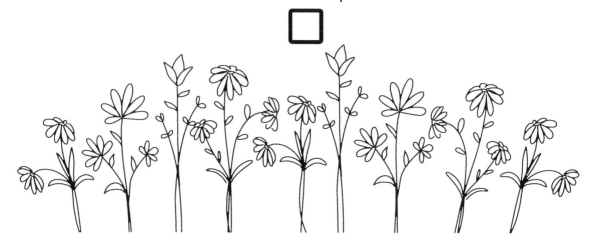

Sunday Reflections

WHEN HAVE YOU FELT LIKE LIFE WAS TOO MUCH TO HANDLE?

_____

_____

_____

_____

HOW DO YOU KNOW GOD IS CLOSE TO THE BROKENHEARTED?

_____

_____

_____

_____

WHEN'S THE LAST TIME YOU RESTED AT THE FOOT OF THE CROSS?

_____

_____

_____

_____

WHAT STEPS CAN YOU TAKE TO SURRENDER YOUR PLANS AND BURDENS?

_____

_____

_____

_____

week seven
SACRIFICE

Happy Monday
Happy Monday
Happy Monday
Happy Monday
Happy Monday
Happy Monday
Happy Monday
Happy Monday

MONDAY GRATITUDE

TODAY I'M FEELING

WHAT'S ON THE SCHEDULE TODAY?

TODAY I'M GRATEFUL FOR

1 _____
2 _____
3 _____

SOMETHING I'M WORKING ON...

_____

MORE OF THIS:

_____
_____
_____
_____

LESS OF THIS:

_____
_____
_____
_____

I AM BLESSED BECAUSE...

_____

I ACCOMPLISHED _____ TODAY:

_____

EMBRACING OUR SUFFERING

I had a slew of things to get done. From emails to appointments to writing and cleaning, I had a productive day mapped out. But our days rarely go as planned, do they? It was a freezing cold day and the heating system went out at my kids' preschool, so he had to be picked up early. My youngest had no desire to nap. After lunches, pick-ups, snacks, and too much driving, it was almost time for dinner. As I stared at my to-do list that was essentially untouched, I could feel myself starting to get frustrated and irritated. My day had been constantly interrupted, I was annoyed, and I got nothing done....according to me.

When we forget our main responsibilities, we lose sight of how God is at work in our lives. We forget our purpose, we forget our role, and we forget to be grateful for the things and people right in front of us.

My main responsibility is not to answer emails. My main responsibility is not writing or making sure my house is spick and span. My focus in this season of life is being a wife and mother. While it can feel like I am making sacrifices, it's the best type of sacrifice because it reaps an eternal reward.

Taking responsibility is often times the hardest when it feels like we're doing chores. Part of taking back our joy is embracing the life God has given us, even in the difficult seasons. It means taking responsibility for things in our life that may be difficult and even involve suffering. But, when we learn to embrace our suffering, we can experience transformational growth because it unites us with Christ in a way we would have never known if we hadn't walked through the pain.

KEY VERSES

Romans 8:18, Colossians 3:23-24, Galatians 6:8-10

wednesday prayer

THURSDAY JOURNAL DAY

PROMPT: AM I BLAMING ANYONE FOR MY CIRCUMSTANCES?

VERSE TO MEDITATE ON

HONEST THOUGHT

CREATIVE FRIDAY

"Tribulation brings about perseverance; and perseverance, proven character; and proven character, hope." Romans 5:3-4 NASB

saturday
action item

MAKE YOUR BED

Checking something off for the day is always beneficial for our mindset. So challenge yourself today. Put on real clothes, put on some makeup, throw in a load of laundry, or eat healthy all day long. Life's battles can be debilitating, but the most important thing is to take the first step today by getting up and making your bed. You got this.

check when complete

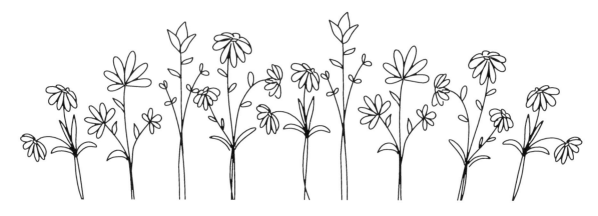

Sunday Reflections

WHAT RESPONSIBILITIES HAS GOD PLACED IN YOUR LIFE?

_____
_____
_____
_____

HAVE YOU EVER EXPERIENCED DEPRESSION? IF SO, WHAT HAS HELPED PULL YOU OUT?

_____
_____
_____
_____

WHAT VERSE CAN YOU CLING TO THROUGH YOUR PAIN TODAY/THIS WEEK?

_____
_____
_____
_____

REMIND YOURSELF OF THE TRUTH OF WHO YOU ARE IN CHRIST. YOU ARE DEEPLY LOVED, VALUED, CALLED TO A PURPOSE...ETC. HOW WILL YOU CHOOSE TO REMEMBER THESE TODAY?

_____
_____
_____
_____

week eight
WORDS

Happy Monday
Happy Monday
Happy Monday
Happy Monday
Happy Monday
Happy Monday
Happy Monday
Happy Monday

MONDAY GRATITUDE

TODAY I'M FEELING

WHAT HAS GOD DONE FOR ME?

TODAY I'M GRATEFUL FOR

1
2
3

SOMETHING I'M WORKING ON...

MORE OF THIS:	LESS OF THIS:

I AM BLESSED BECAUSE...

tuesday
DEVOTIONAL

WORDS, MINDSET, AND COMPLAINING

It had been a long week. A stomach bug had just torn through our family and I had finally managed to get a few minutes of alone time and take a hot shower. It was a moment of peace. I was clean, everyone was on the mend and beginning to feel better, and I was most grateful for the direction God had recently given our family. Things were looking up. Moments later, my phone buzzed with the arrival of a new text message. As I read the text, I became riled up and the peace I had felt was shattered. Who does this person think they are? Why is this happening? Do they understand how hurtful this is?

I thought the turbulence in our life had begun to smooth out, but when I received this text it seemed to stir the pot again. I was so hurt. I was confused and didn't know how to respond. I prayed and vented to the Lord. I talked with my husband. I even called a friend.

As I was hanging up the phone, my husband walked back into the room where I was sitting. My heart was racing and I was angry. We talked for a second about the circumstances when he interrupted me and said, "This is always what the enemy does when things are going well."

Bingo! Why was I so surprised that this was happening right now? God had just recently given me and my husband such clarity and direction on something that we had long prayed for. Our family was all healing and almost through a long bout of sickness. I had much to be thankful for and that is what I needed to remember.

Let's not allow the enemy to use circumstances to throw us off and get us spiraling downwards. As our words and our thoughts reflect the condition of our hearts, let's stop complaining and be rooted in thankfulness this week, regardless of what life throws at us.

KEY VERSES
Matthew 7:24-27, Psalm 71:8, Psalm 118:1

wednesday prayer

THURSDAY JOURNAL DAY

PROMPT: DO I COMPLAIN WHEN THINGS DON'T GO MY WAY?

VERSE TO MEDITATE ON

HONEST THOUGHT

CREATIVE FRIDAY

"Do all things without complaining and disputing." Philippians 2:14 NKJV

saturday
action item

MAKE PRAYER YOUR MISSION

Throughout the day today, focus on prayer. I love that no matter who doesn't respond or listen, God always does.

"Rejoice always, pray without ceasing, give thanks in all circumstances; for this is the will of God in Christ Jesus for you."
1 Thessalonians 5:16-18 ESV

check when complete

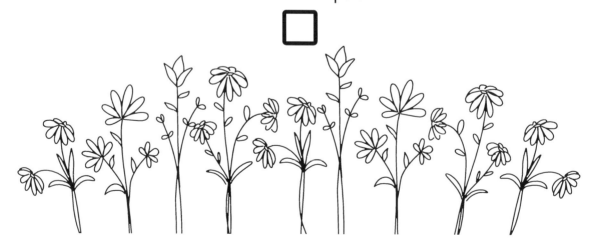

Sunday Reflections

DO YOU COMPLAIN MORE THAN YOU GIVE PRAISE? IF SO, HOW CAN YOU
CHANGE YOUR MINDSET?

_____

_____

_____

_____

THINK ABOUT THE ROOT OF YOUR COMPLAINTS. DO YOU FEEL TAKEN CARE
OF? DO YOU FEEL YOUR LIFE IS TOO HARD? DO YOU FEEL ALONE?

_____

_____

_____

_____

IT'S OK TO BE REAL AND HONEST, BUT HOW CAN YOU BE ON GUARD SO THAT
YOUR COMPLAINTS DON'T SPIRAL DOWNWARD?

_____

_____

_____

_____

DO YOU BELIEVE GOD HAS GOOD THINGS SPECIFICALLY FOR YOU? HOW DO
YOU KNOW? IS GOD'S "GOOD" FOR YOU DIFFERENT THAN WHAT YOU THINK IS
GOOD? UNPACK THIS TODAY.

_____

_____

_____

_____

week nine
TRUST

Happy Monday

Happy Monday

Happy Monday

Happy Monday

Happy Monday

Happy Monday

Happy Monday

Happy Monday

MONDAY GRATITUDE

TODAY I'M FEELING

WHAT CAN I LET GO OF TODAY?

TODAY I'M GRATEFUL FOR

1
2
3

SOMETHING I'M WORKING ON...

MORE OF THIS:	LESS OF THIS:

I AM BLESSED BECAUSE...

tuesday
DEVOTIONAL

CONTROLLING

First, it was an email from the school nurse with the subject line "Lice breakout." My anxiety began to rise. Then, we discovered that our dog had fleas. To top it all off, a stomach bug then infected our home. My anxiety peaked. I'm not sure what it is about small bugs and germs that I find so creepy and disgusting, but they drive me into a full-on, psychotic house-cleaning spree. Can anyone else relate? Maybe it's because I feel like everything around me is pure madness and cleaning is the only way that I can get control of things. I steam-cleaned our carpets and couch, scrubbed all the baseboards, and almost broke our washer because I sanitized virtually anything that was made of fabric.

When things are out of control, I take it upon myself to fix everything. A few days after my cleaning spree, would you be surprised to learn that another one of my kids got sick? I gave my husband a look of utter despair and said, "This was not supposed to happen! I did absolutely everything I could to prevent this!" I finally started to see that I cannot do it all.

We often try to exert control over our lives to an insane degree, especially when things aren't going the way we had planned. But we need to release control and live with open hands, knowing that our sovereign Lord is working and has a plan for us. Now, don't get me wrong, we do have some responsibility as Jesus isn't going to come down and do our laundry. But our God has all the authority and power and we can trust Him, even when life just doesn't seem to be going our way.

KEY VERSES
Proverbs 3:5-6, Psalm 135:6-7, Philippians 4:6-7

wednesday prayer

THURSDAY JOURNAL DAY

PROMPT: DO I BELIEVE GOD HAS EVERYTHING UNDER CONTROL?

VERSE TO MEDITATE ON

HONEST THOUGHT

CREATIVE FRIDAY

"May the God of hope fill you with all joy and peace as you trust in him, so
that you may overflow with hope by the
power of the Holy Spirit."
Romans 15:13 NIV

saturday
action item

IDENTIFY IT

When our lives are filled with chaos, sometimes we
feel the need to control everything we can. Today,
identify one thing you're having trouble trusting God
with and write it on a small piece of paper. Spend
15 minutes lifting it up prayer. When you're done,
crumple it up and throw it away.
Trust God with it all.

check when complete

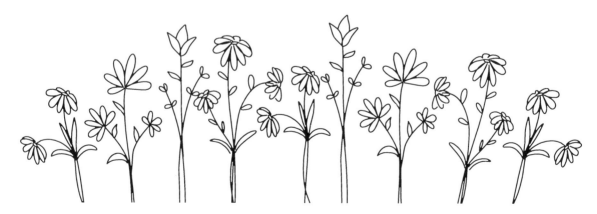

Sunday Reflections

WHEN WAS THE LAST TIME YOU FELT LIKE YOU WERE STUCK BETWEEN BOTH PAIN AND JOY?

_____

_____

_____

_____

ARE YOU GOOD AT TRUSTING OTHERS AND THE LORD? IF NOT, WHAT IS HOLDING YOU BACK?

_____

_____

_____

_____

THINK OF A VERSE TODAY/THIS WEEK ON TRUSTING AND MEMORIZE IT.

_____

_____

_____

_____

LIFE IS SO MUCH BETTER WHEN GOD IS IN CONTROL. DO YOU HAVE TROUBLE BELIEVING THAT? WHY?

_____

_____

_____

week ten
CONFIDENCE

Happy Monday
Happy Monday
Happy Monday
Happy Monday
Happy Monday
Happy Monday
Happy Monday
Happy Monday

MONDAY GRATITUDE

TODAY I'M FEELING

DOES SOCIAL MEDIA BENEFIT ME?

TODAY I'M GRATEFUL FOR

1 ....
2 ....
3 ....

SOMETHING I'M WORKING ON...

MORE OF THIS:

LESS OF THIS:

I AM BLESSED BECAUSE...

OUR WORST DAY AND THEIR BEST DAY

I had been waiting for the bestsellers-list to be published for over a week and was checking the website multiple times a day. I thought that there was a small chance that I could make the list. Everyone loves a good underdog story like David defeating Goliath, the last becoming first. However, sometimes God's plan for our lives does not fit our vision. Yes, He wants good things for us. But our definition of good doesn't always match His. Sometimes "good" means enduring suffering and learning things the hard way.

When I saw that my book wasn't on the list, I was bummed out. Why would God call me to write something that pushed people to the gospel and not make it successful? Why did He want me to pour out my heart and take over two years creating something that wouldn't be a bestseller? My idea of success was limited to what I thought was best.

The truth is that God has such a beautiful plan for us when we're in step with Him and guided by the Spirit. Part of that is being content with what is right in front of you, your daily manna, and not measuring yourself against others. We have all seen the person blessed with worldly success that ends in ruin. We need to remind ourselves that we serve a loving and faithful God who has a glorious eternity planned for us that even the best version of our lives can't compete with! There is so much goodness right in front of us if we just surrender and stop comparing our own journey with those around us.

In the end, we're comparing our worst days to an idealized version of someone else's best. Let's break that cycle today.

KEY VERSES

Philippians 4:11-12, Matthew 6:11, Ephesians 2:8-10

wednesday prayer

THURSDAY JOURNAL DAY

PROMPT: DO YOU EVER FEEL FORGOTTEN BY GOD?

VERSE TO MEDITATE ON

HONEST THOUGHT

CREATIVE FRIDAY

"I praise you because I am fearfully and wonderfully made; your works are wonderful, I know that full well." Psalm 139:14 NIV

saturday
action item

WRITE OUT A TRUTH STATEMENT

Write out a truth-filled Bible verse, statement,
phrase, or something that encourages you to keep
going on a sticky note today. Plaster that thing
where you spend most of your time and meditate
on its value today.

"So if the Son sets you free, you are truly free."
John 8:36 NLT

check when complete

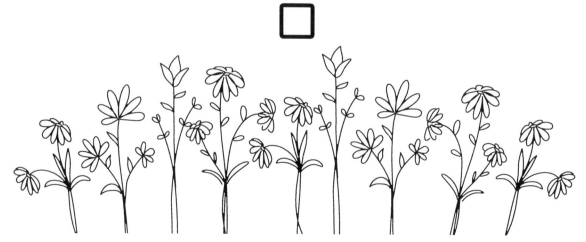

Sunday Reflections

DO YOU COMPARE YOURSELF TO OTHERS ON SOCIAL MEDIA? IF SO, WHY?

_____

_____

_____

WHAT STEPS CAN YOU TAKE TO LIVE A LIFE OF CONTENTMENT AND PEACE?

_____

_____

_____

WHO CAN YOU CELEBRATE AND UPLIFT TODAY THAT NEEDS YOUR SUPPORT?

_____

_____

_____

STRIVING TOWARDS CHRIST IS THE ONLY STRIVING THAT IS WORTH IT. REMIND YOURSELF OF WHAT'S RIGHT IN FRONT OF YOU AND ALL THAT GOD HAS GIVEN YOU.

_____

_____

_____

week eleven
PURPOSE

Happy Monday
Happy Monday
Happy Monday
Happy Monday
Happy Monday
Happy Monday
Happy Monday
Happy Monday

MONDAY GRATITUDE

TODAY I'M FEELING

DO I HAVE A PURPOSE?

TODAY I'M GRATEFUL FOR

1
2
3

SOMETHING I'M WORKING ON...

MORE OF THIS:

LESS OF THIS:

I AM BLESSED BECAUSE...

TOMORROW I LOOK FORWARD TO

tuesday
DEVOTIONAL

PURPOSE IN PAIN

Someone asked me the other day, "Do you believe there is a purpose to everything you've walked through?" I had to sit and contemplate that for a while. On one hand, I know I may never have an answer for some of the most painful things that I've walked through if it's not part of God's plan. But on the other hand, I believe that God, in His goodness and faithfulness and grace, does not waste a thing. The true meaning of "working things together for my good" started to actually make sense when I abandoned my own definition of "good" and embraced the Lord's version, His "good, pleasing, and perfect" will for my life.

And it WAS better.

What you need to know today as we finish up our last week together is that YOU have a purpose. It's not about the pain or the trauma or whatever the enemy's attempt to steal your joy. Instead, it's about how YOU are still breathing, still alive, and still have a purpose specifically tailored to you because you are unique and created in His image. Offer up whatever you have to the Lord and allow him to multiply it. Who knows? He may feed thousands with your small offering...

KEY VERSES
Mark 12: 41-44, Matthew 14: 13-21, John 3:16-17, Romans 12:2

wednesday prayer

THURSDAY JOURNAL DAY

PROMPT: IS THERE PURPOSE IN MY PAIN?

VERSE TO MEDITATE ON

HONEST THOUGHT

CREATIVE FRIDAY

"Go therefore and make disciples of all the nations, baptizing them in the name of the Father and of the Son and of the Holy Spirit, teaching them to observe all things that I have commanded you."
Matthew 28:19-20 NKJV

saturday
action item

TELL SOMEONE YOU LOVE THEM

Remind your spouse, best friend, family member, or child how much you love and appreciate them. Everyone could use some extra love today. People need to be reminded that they are valued and loved. I sure do!

check when complete

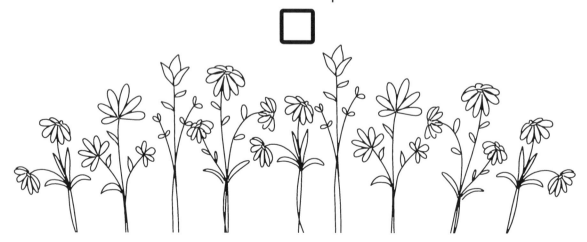

Sunday Reflections

WHAT KEEPS YOU GOING WHEN YOU'RE IN THE MIDDLE OF PAIN?

_____

_____

_____

GOD HAS ALWAYS COME THROUGH, AND HE WILL AGAIN AND AGAIN. WHAT VERSE CAN YOU MEMORIZE AND CLING TO TODAY/THIS WEEK FOR COMFORT IN YOUR PAIN?

_____

_____

_____

HOW HAS GOD USED THE DIFFICULTIES YOU'VE GONE THROUGH?

_____

_____

_____

PRAISE GOD FOR ALL THAT HE'S DONE IN YOUR LIFE!

_____

_____

_____

You did it!

I hope and pray our time together was beneficial in so many ways. I'd love to hear how God used this resource to restore your joy as you continue to fight for purpose when life is more than you can handle.

For more information or to book Nicole for your next women's event, scan the code below.

Praying for you!

scan me!

About

Through her authenticity and the sharing of her own struggles and pain, Nicole encourages women to keep going when all seems lost. She believes that it's possible to find lasting joy and purpose in Christ and that He is good no matter what life brings our way. Nicole and her husband, Andrew, have 4 kids and reside in North Carolina. They love being outdoors, baking chocolate chip cookies, and playing sports. Connect with her on Instagram @nicole.jacobsmeyer and her website nicolejacobsmeyer.com

join our community!

Take Back Your Joy

Fighting for Purpose When Life Is More Than You Can Handle

Now Available!

Crowned Free

We are on a mission to end human trafficking through
ethical fashion and gifts.
Scan the QR code below to learn more!

Made in the USA
Columbia, SC
29 March 2025

55864567R00067